A Mammoth Task

Explorer Challenge

Find out what Mum picks up
by the cliffs ...

OXFORD
UNIVERSITY PRESS

Wilf and Wilma were fed up.

"This is not much of a holiday," moaned Wilma.

"It's rained every day so far and it's been so windy."

2

"Look on the bright side," said Dad. "We've got the beach all to ourselves and the wind is great for blowing these windmills."

"I'm feeling quite chilly in this wind," said Mum. "Come on! Let's go and get a hot drink."

"I'd like a hot chocolate," said Wilf.

By the evening, the wind was even stronger.
Giant waves crashed against the wall.
"It's going to be a stormy night," said Mum.

The next day, the storm was over and the sun was out. People were clearing up after the storm. The waves had left pebbles and seaweed everywhere.

6

The sea had crashed against the cliffs all along the beach. In the far distance, a big part of the cliff had fallen down.

"These cliffs are not made of hard rock," said Dad. "If a rough sea crashes into them, they can collapse."

Wilma saw something sticking out of the cliff.
"What's that?" she asked. "It looks like a giant bone."
"I think it *is* a bone," said Mum.

"I wonder if it's from a dinosaur," said Wilf.
"It would be exciting to find dinosaur bones."
"I think I'll make a phone call," said Dad.

By the afternoon, a team of experts had come to look at the bone.

"This is exciting," said a man. "It looks like the leg bone of a mammoth."

"It's a steppe mammoth," the man went on. "It's a sort of mammoth, but it's quite like the elephants that live now. This leg bone is about four hundred thousand years old."

"So it's not a woolly mammoth?" asked Wilf.

"No, it's not," said the man. "It's even bigger than a woolly mammoth. They lived at different times. They are both extinct now. Being extinct means they no longer exist."

A fence was put round the base of the cliff.

"We need to dig out the leg bone gently," said the man. "Then we will excavate to find the rest of the mammoth."

The next day, Wilf and Wilma went to the beach. A lot of bones lay on a plastic sheet but, most exciting of all, the skull of the mammoth had been excavated.

"It's huge," said Wilf, "but it only has one tusk."
"We may still find the other tusk," the man said.
Then there was a shout. The tusk had been found!

"Will you put all the bones together and make a proper skeleton?" asked Wilf.

"I'm afraid not," said the man. "The bones are much too fragile."

Wilf took lots of photos of the bones.
"I'm going to find out all about mammoths,"
he said. "It's a shame they can't make up the
mammoth's skeleton."

"Look at this," said Mum, the next day. "We are in the newspaper, on the front page. It says, 'The family saw the bone of a prehistoric animal'."

Wilf bought an extra copy of the newspaper.

"So it was you who found the mammoth bone," said the shopkeeper.

"Yes!" said Wilf. "I am going to cut this page out and put it in my scrapbook."

After the holiday, Wilf worked hard on his project.

"The steppe mammoth was enormous," he said. "The male weighed about ten tonnes and was over four metres tall."

"How much taller is that than us?" asked Wilma.

Dad showed a picture of the mammoth to some people he worked with.

"It's a pity the experts can't put the skeleton back together," he said. "But I have an idea and I need you to help me."

Dad told Mrs May about his plan.
"What a great idea!" said Mrs May.

Dad took his picture to a timber yard.
"You'll need a lot of wood to make a thing that big," said a man.

Dad took his picture to a workshop.
"This looks interesting. We'll do it," said a man.

Dad and his workmates went to the school field.
They put up a big frame.

At school, Wilf gave a talk about the mammoth.
He told his class how Wilma had seen the bone
on the beach. He showed them lots of pictures.

24

Anneena thanked Wilf for his interesting talk.
Then Mrs May said, "Now we are going outside.
There is a big surprise waiting for us."

What a surprise it was! Wilf's dad and his workmates had made a wooden outline of a mammoth. It was held up by a metal frame.

"It's just massive!" said Biff. "I never thought they could be so huge. Imagine how much grass they munched!"

The children had their photos taken next to the mammoth's front leg.

"This is just amazing," said Nadim.

"Thanks Dad," said Wilf. "I love it!"
"It was a mammoth task," joked Dad.
"And a mammoth tusk!" said Wilf.

Retell the Story

Look at the pictures and retell the story in your own words.

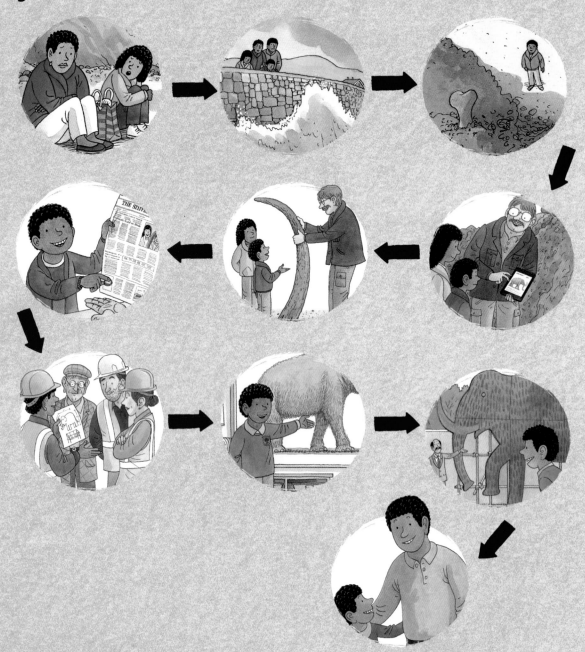

Look Back, Explorers

What were the people clearing up after the storm?

How old was the bone?

How do you think Dad felt about leaving the beach where he had put up the windmills?

What did Dad mean when he said it was 'a mammoth task' to build the mammoth?

Imagine that you were there when the bone was found. What questions would you ask the expert?

Did you find out what Mum picked up by the cliffs?

Explorer Challenge: a fossil of a fern plant (page 17)

What's Next, Explorers?

Now you know about an extinct mammoth, find out about more extinct giants ...

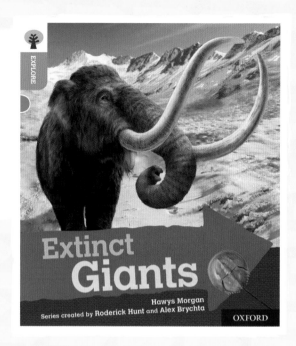

Explorer Challenge
for *Extinct Giants*

Find out which animal had teeth like these ...